Fun Food for Children

Juliet Sykes

First published in 1998 for
Tesco Stores Limited
by Brilliant Books Ltd
84-86 Regent Street
London W1R 6DD

Text and photographs © 1998 Brilliant Books Ltd

Origination by Colourpath Ltd, London
Printed and bound by Jarrold Book Printing,
Thetford, England

Fun Food for Children

Juliet Sykes

TESCO

About the author

After cooking for a children's theatre for several years, Juliet Sykes now specialises in conjuring up new ways to make children's food more appealing and fun. Juliet tries out all her ideas on her own three children.

Photographer	Peter Cassidy
Home economist	Bridget Sargeson
Stylist	Roisin Nield
Recipes tested by	Terry Farris
	Anne Sheasby

CONTENTS

INTRODUCTION

The recipes in this book have been created and photographed specially for Tesco. They have been thoroughly tested and all the ingredients are normally available at larger Tesco stores, when in season. There is no need for any special kitchen equipment.

Using the recipes

1 Both metric and imperial weights and measures are given, except for goods sold in standard size packaging, such as cans. As conversions are not always exact, you should follow either the metric or the imperial throughout each recipe where possible.

2 British standard level spoon measurements are used. A tablespoon measure is equivalent to 15ml; a teaspoon measure is equivalent to 5ml.

3 Dishes cooked in the oven should be placed in the centre, unless otherwise stated. Tesco advises that all meat, poultry, fish and eggs should be cooked thoroughly. Poultry juices should run clear when the flesh is pierced with a skewer at its thickest point.

4 None of the recipes in this book contains nuts. However, it is advisable to check the labelling of any commercially prepared products to ensure that they do not contain nuts or nut derivatives, which should not be eaten by children, people who have an allergic reaction to nuts, or women who are pregnant or breastfeeding. Dishes including honey should not be eaten by children under 12 months.

5 Seasoning with pepper is to suit your palate. Tesco advises that dishes prepared for children should not contain salt as a seasoning, therefore no extra salt has been included in these recipes.

6 Vegetables and fruits are medium-sized, unless otherwise stated. When cooking or serving vegetables or fruits with their skins on, make sure that they are thoroughly rinsed.

7 The fat and calorie content of each recipe is given. The figures are for one serving only.

8 Each recipe has a simplicity rating of 1, 2 or 3 chef's hats. Recipes with 1 hat are easy; those with 2 or 3 will require a little more effort.

PIG SWILL

Serves 2

Preparation 20 mins

Cooking 40 mins

Calories 429

Fat 25g

Simplicity

1 Heat 1 tablespoon of the oil in a heavy-based saucepan, then add the onion, celery and leek. Cook, covered, for 5 minutes or until softened, stirring occasionally. Add the tomatoes, carrot, parsnip and potato, then cook for 3-4 minutes longer.

2 Pour the vegetable stock into the pan and season. Bring to the boil, cover, then simmer for 30 minutes, or until the vegetables are tender. Remove from the heat and purée the soup with a hand blender until thick but still chunky, or mash with a potato masher. Add the frankfurter pieces, if using, to the purée and heat through for 3 minutes.

3 Meanwhile, use a small pig-shaped pastry cutter to stamp out 6 'pigs' from the bread. Heat the remaining oil in a frying pan, then fry the bread pigs for 2-3 minutes on each side until golden. Drain on kitchen towels. Serve the croûtons with the soup.

Ingredients
2 tbsp vegetable oil
1 small onion, chopped
1 stick celery, chopped
1 small leek, sliced
227g can chopped tomatoes
1 small carrot, chopped
1 small parsnip, chopped
1 small potato, diced
300ml (½ pint) vegetable stock
Black pepper
2 frankfurters, cut into small pieces (optional)
2 slices wholemeal bread

Little pigs snuffling around in a trough of vegetables will captivate any small child. The chunky soup is delicious and easy to make, but you will need a pig-shaped cutter.

WILD FLOWER MEADOW SALAD

Simplicity

Serves 2

Preparation 15 mins

Cooking 10 mins

Calories 352

Fat 30g

---

1 medium egg

50g (2oz) mixed salad leaves

6 baby corn, thinly sliced into rounds

6 cherry tomatoes, halved

40g (1½oz) seedless white grapes

1 small red eating apple, cored and diced

50g (2oz) Gruyère, thinly sliced and cut into leaf shapes

For the dressing

1 tsp Dijon mustard

2 tbsp olive oil

1 tbsp wine vinegar

2 tbsp natural yogurt

Black pepper

1 Hard-boil the egg for 10 minutes in a small saucepan of boiling water. Cool under cold running water, peel off the shell, then cut into sixths. Arrange the salad leaves in bowls and scatter over the baby corn, tomatoes, grapes, apple, Gruyère and hard-boiled egg.

2 To make the dressing, mix together the mustard, oil, vinegar, yogurt and seasoning. Drizzle over the salad.

This colourful selection of grapes, baby corn and cherry tomatoes makes a great imaginary flower meadow. But you can use whatever fruit and vegetables you've got.

EGGS IN PONCHOS

Serves 2

Preparation 20 mins

Cooking 10 mins

Calories 568

Fat 42g

Simplicity

1 First make the guacamole. Place the avocado, tomato, spring onions, lime juice and coriander, if using, in a bowl. Mash with a fork to combine, then cover and set aside.

2 Place the bacon in a frying pan and fry in its own fat for 3 minutes or until crisp, then set aside. Mix the eggs and milk together with a fork, then season with pepper. Melt the butter in a non-stick saucepan. Add the egg mixture and cook, stirring, for 3 minutes or until the egg is scrambled and well cooked. Gently stir in the bacon pieces.

3 Meanwhile, heat the chilli beans in a saucepan for 4-5 minutes. Place a frying pan over a medium heat, then warm the tortillas, one at a time, for 15 seconds on each side. Transfer to plates, top with the scrambled egg and chilli beans, then wrap each tortilla loosely around its filling. Serve with the guacamole and tomato wedges.

2 rashers back bacon, cut into small pieces

3 medium eggs

2 tbsp full-fat milk

Black pepper

25g (1oz) butter

4 tbsp canned chilli beans

2 wheat tortillas

For the guacamole

1 ripe avocado, stoned, peeled and chopped

1 small tomato, chopped, plus 1 tomato, cut into wedges, to garnish

2 spring onions, finely chopped

Juice of ½ lime

½ tsp chopped fresh coriander (optional)

Tortillas are filled with a delicious combination of scrambled egg and chilli beans. Creamy guacamole completes this colourful Mexican-inspired dish.

H I D E A N D S E E K

Simplicity

Serves 2

Preparation 25 mins

Cooking 1 hr 10 mins

Calories 478

Fat 28g

2 medium baking potatoes

Butter or sunflower oil
for greasing

2 rashers back bacon, cut into
small pieces

50g (2oz) Red Leicester, grated

1 tbsp crème fraîche

2 tsp snipped fresh chives

Black pepper

For the coleslaw

100g (3½oz) red cabbage,
shredded

2 spring onions, chopped

1 eating apple, cored
and chopped

1 small carrot, grated

2 tbsp mayonnaise

1 Preheat the oven to 220°C/425°F/Gas Mark 7. Rub the skins of the potatoes with butter or oil. Put the potatoes in the oven and cook for 1 hour or until soft in the centre.

2 Place the bacon in a frying pan and cook in its own fat for 3 minutes or until crisp, then set aside. To make the coleslaw, combine the cabbage, spring onions, apple, carrot and mayonnaise, and refrigerate until needed.

3 When the potatoes are cooked, slice the top off each one and reserve. Scoop out the centres and place in a bowl with the Red Leicester, crème fraîche, chives and bacon pieces. Mix well with a fork and season. Pile the mixture back into the empty potato skins and return to the oven for 5 minutes to heat through. Replace the reserved potato tops over the filled potatoes and serve with the coleslaw.

When children lift the potato lids, they'll discover a delicious, creamy, cheese and bacon filling. Use any leftover potato mixture as a base for making fish cakes.

SHEEP DIP

Serves 4

Preparation 10 mins

plus 20 mins cooling

Cooking 25 mins

Calories 428

Fat 29g

Simplicity

1 Preheat the oven to 200°C/400°F/Gas Mark 6. Roll out the pastry thinly on a floured surface. Stamp out 8-10 sheep shapes, using a 5cm (2in) fluted pastry cutter for the bodies and a 3cm (1¼in) cutter for the heads. Cut out 2.5cm (1in) strips for the legs. Brush with milk and stick together, then place on a baking sheet. Bake for 10 minutes or until golden. Transfer to a rack to cool for 20 minutes.

2 Meanwhile, make the dip. Melt the butter in a saucepan over a low heat. Sprinkle in the flour and cook for 1 minute, stirring. Remove the pan from the heat, then gradually add the milk, whisking all the time. Return to the heat and cook gently, stirring, for 3-4 minutes or until thickened. Gradually stir in the juice, then simmer for 2 minutes, stirring. Add the cheese, stir until melted, season, then keep warm.

3 Boil the cauliflower for 5 minutes or until tender. Pour the dip into a bowl and sprinkle with spring onion. Serve with the cauliflower and pastry 'sheep'.

For the 'sheep'

175g (6oz) shortcrust pastry

Milk for brushing

1 small cauliflower, cut into florets

For the dip

15g (½oz) butter

15g (½oz) plain flour

150ml (¼ pint) full-fat milk

100ml (4fl oz) apple juice

125g (4oz) mature Cheddar, grated

Black pepper

1 spring onion, finely chopped

These fluffy sheep shapes transform cauliflower cheese into a magical meal for small children. This is sure to be a winning combination at birthday parties.

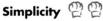

GIANT CATHERINE WHEELS

Simplicity

Makes 10

Preparation 15 mins
plus 20 mins chilling

Cooking 20 mins

Calories 267 each

Fat 19g each

400g (14oz) shortcrust pastry

Plain flour for dusting

100g (3½oz) mature
Cheddar, grated

2 tbsp freshly grated Parmesan

2 tbsp tomato purée

2 tbsp pesto

1 medium egg, beaten,
for glazing

Vegetable oil for greasing

1 Preheat the oven to 190°C/375°F/Gas Mark 5. Roll out the pastry on a floured surface and cut to make 2 rectangles measuring 20 x 25cm (8 x 10in). Mix together the Cheddar and Parmesan, then set aside.

2 Spread 1 sheet of pastry with the tomato purée. Place the second sheet of pastry on top, spread with the pesto, then sprinkle with the cheese. Roll up the pastry from the shorter side with the filling inside. Brush the roll with the egg and refrigerate for 20 minutes.

3 Cut the roll into 1cm (½in) slices and place on greased baking sheets. Bake for 20 minutes or until golden. Leave to cool slightly on wire racks.

An indoor sparkler fizzing in the middle of these tasty
tomato and pesto pastry swirls will cause a sensation!
But – as always – take great care with fireworks.

PRETTY POSY PIZZAS

Serves 2

Preparation 15 mins

Cooking 45 mins

Calories 459

Fat 22g

Simplicity

1 Place the onion, tomatoes, tomato purée, basil and pepper to taste in a saucepan. Simmer for 20 minutes, stirring occasionally, or until thickened.

2 Meanwhile, make the pizza bases. Put the flour and oregano into a large bowl, season, then add 1 tablespoon of the oil and 4 tablespoons of cold water. Mix with your hands to make a soft dough.

3 Turn the dough out onto a floured board. Knead for 1 minute, until smooth, then halve it and roll each piece into a 13cm (5in) round. Heat the remaining oil in a large, non-stick frying pan and gently cook the bases, one at a time, for 5 minutes on each side or until golden.

4 Preheat the grill to high. Spread the tomato sauce over the bases. Make a flower shape on the top of each pizza using pepperoni slices for petals and a slice of mozzarella for the centre. Place under the grill for 2 minutes to melt the cheese. Garnish with basil.

For the pizzas

125g (4oz) self-raising flour, sifted

1 tsp dried oregano

Black pepper

2 tbsp olive oil

For the topping

1 small onion, finely chopped

227g can chopped tomatoes

1 tsp tomato purée

1 tsp chopped fresh basil, plus leaves to garnish

Black pepper

9 small slices pepperoni, halved

2 slices fresh mozzarella

These homemade pizzas are pretty and delicious, and really quick to make. Children can decorate their own pizzas with a variety of their favourite toppings.

PICK UP STICKS

Simplicity

Serves 2

Preparation 15 mins
plus 1 hr marinating

Cooking 12 mins

Calories 133

Fat 5g

¼ red pepper and ¼ yellow pepper, cut into small chunks

4 button mushrooms, quartered

1 small courgette, thickly sliced and halved lengthways

100g (3½oz) Quorn, cubed

For the marinade

1 tbsp lemon juice

1 tsp clear honey

2 tbsp light soy sauce

Black pepper

For the dipping sauce

1 tsp olive oil

1 small clove garlic, chopped

3 tbsp plum sauce

1 tsp soft light brown sugar

100ml (4fl oz) vegetable stock

1 Soak 6 wooden skewers in water for 10 minutes to prevent them burning under the grill. To make the marinade, mix together the lemon juice, honey, soy sauce and pepper in a large, non-metallic dish. Add the red and yellow peppers, mushrooms, courgette and Quorn and stir to coat. Place in the fridge for 1 hour to marinate.

2 Preheat the grill to medium. Thread the vegetables and Quorn onto the skewers. Grill for 6 minutes, turning the skewers occasionally, until evenly cooked.

3 Meanwhile, make the dipping sauce. Heat the oil in a saucepan. Add the garlic and cook, stirring, for 1 minute or until softened. Stir in the plum sauce, sugar and stock and boil rapidly for 5 minutes or until the sauce has reduced and thickened slightly. Serve with the kebabs.

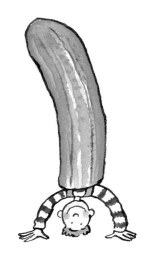

For a main meal, serve these vegetable kebabs on a bed of crisp salad leaves with plain rice or noodles and dress with the fruity dipping sauce.

PLOUGH THE FIELDS AND SCATTER

Serves 2

Preparation 10 mins

Cooking 45 mins

Calories 565

Fat 36g

Simplicity

1 Cook the potatoes in boiling water for 15 minutes or until tender, then drain. Mash with the milk and half the butter. Meanwhile, heat the oil in a heavy-based frying pan, add the onion and garlic and cook for 5 minutes or until softened. Add the carrot and cook for another 3 minutes to soften slightly.

2 Add the minced lamb and herbs to the onion and garlic and break up the mince with a wooden spoon. Cook for 10 minutes or until the mince has browned. Season, then add the stock and simmer, uncovered, for 20 minutes or until most of the liquid has evaporated. Add the Worcestershire sauce.

3 Preheat the grill to high. Mix together the lamb mixture and potatoes, then place in a flameproof dish. Sprinkle with the breadcrumbs and cheese. Drag the handle of a wooden spoon along the top to make furrows, then grill for 3-4 minutes, until golden. Meanwhile, fry the peas in the remaining butter for 1-2 minutes. Scatter over the 'field' with the chives.

125g (4oz) potatoes, diced
1 tbsp full-fat milk
25g (1oz) butter
2 tsp sunflower oil
1 onion, chopped
1 small clove garlic, crushed
1 carrot, diced
225g (8oz) minced lamb
2 tsp mixed fresh herbs, such as thyme and rosemary
Black pepper
150ml (¼ pint) lamb stock
Dash of Worcestershire sauce
2 tbsp fresh breadcrumbs
25g (1oz) mature Cheddar, grated
40g (1½oz) frozen peas
2 tsp snipped fresh chives

This meal-in-a-dish can be served on its own, but if you get carried away you can complete the rural scene by adding a hedgerow made from steamed broccoli florets.

POT PLANTS

Simplicity

Serves 2

Preparation 10 mins

Cooking 30 mins

Calories 306

Fat 18g

1 red and 1 yellow pepper

1 tbsp balsamic vinegar

2 tbsp olive oil

2 baby corns

1 small onion, chopped

1 small clove garlic, chopped

75g (3oz) minced lamb

1 tsp tomato purée

25g (1oz) bulgar wheat

150ml (¼ pint) lamb stock

25g (1oz) frozen peas

25g (1oz) ready-to-eat dried apricots, chopped

1 tsp ground coriander

Black pepper

Watercress sprigs to garnish

1 Preheat the oven to 200°C/400°F/Gas Mark 6. Slice off and discard the tops of the peppers and deseed. Square off the bottoms and stand on a baking sheet. Sprinkle with the balsamic vinegar and 1 tablespoon of the oil. Cook for 15 minutes, then add the baby corns to the sheet. Cook for 5-10 minutes, until everything is tender.

2 Meanwhile, heat the remaining oil in a large saucepan, add the onion and garlic and fry for 5 minutes or until softened. Add the minced lamb and cook for 5 minutes or until browned. Stir in the tomato purée, bulgar wheat, stock, peas, apricots and coriander, then season. Bring to the boil, then simmer for 15 minutes or until the stock has been absorbed, stirring occasionally.

3 Place the peppers on plates and fill with the lamb mixture. Insert a baby corn and watercress sprigs into the top of each one for the pot plants.

This is a great way to get children to eat fresh vegetables. But if they don't like peppers, you can always use two hollowed-out large beefsteak tomatoes instead.

JACK AND THE BEAN PORK

Serves 2

Preparation 15 mins

Cooking 35 mins

Calories 472

Fat 22g

Simplicity

1 Cook the potatoes and carrot in boiling water for 10-15 minutes, until tender, then drain well and mash with the butter and pepper.

2 Heat the oil in a saucepan. Fry the spring onions and garlic for 3 minutes or until softened. Add the sausages and cook for 10-15 minutes, until browned and cooked through. Stir in the ratatouille and beans and heat through, then season again.

3 Preheat the grill to medium. Transfer the sausage mixture to a flameproof dish, top with the mash and sprinkle with cheese. Grill for 3 minutes or until the cheese browns. Meanwhile, cook the courgette strips and mangetout in boiling water for 2 minutes to soften. Arrange the courgette strips on top of the pie in the shape of a beanstalk, using the mangetout as leaves.

225g (8oz) potatoes, diced

1 small carrot, diced

Knob of butter

Black pepper

1 tsp vegetable oil

3 spring onions, chopped

1 small clove garlic, crushed

8 cocktail sausages or 4 pork sausages, halved widthways

200g (7oz) canned ratatouille

125g (4oz) canned mixed beans, rinsed and drained

25g (1oz) Cheddar, grated

Thin strips of courgette and whole mangetout

This comforting dish of mixed beans and vegetables will transport children to the fairytale world of giants and Daisy the cow. Perhaps the beans are magic!

STICKS AND STONES

Simplicity

Serves 2

Preparation 10 mins

Cooking 45 mins

Calories 400

Fat 33g

For the 'sticks'

2 tsp vegetable oil

1 small red onion, thinly sliced

1 tsp soft dark brown sugar

For the 'stones'

125g (4oz) lean minced pork

50g (2oz) rindless back bacon, finely chopped

1 tbsp vegetable oil

For the tomato sauce

227g can chopped tomatoes

Pinch of dried oregano

1 tsp sun-dried tomato purée

Black pepper

1 First make the sauce. Put the tomatoes, oregano, tomato purée and pepper into a saucepan. Cook gently for 20 minutes or until the sauce thickens, stirring occasionally.

2 Meanwhile, make the sticky caramelised onions. Heat the oil in a heavy-based frying pan, add the onion and cook gently for 10 minutes or until softened, stirring occasionally. Add the sugar and cook gently for 2-3 minutes, stirring, until brown and sticky. Remove from the pan and set aside.

3 Make the 'stones'. Mix the pork and bacon in a bowl and roll into 8 walnut-sized balls, using your hands. Heat the oil in a frying pan and cook the meatballs for 15 minutes, turning occasionally, until cooked and browned. Pour the tomato sauce over and simmer for 5 minutes, then transfer to bowls. Top each serving with a spoonful of onions.

Sticky caramelised onions and meatball 'stones' won't break any bones and will make supper time fun. Serve them with rice to soak up the thick tomato sauce.

NOODLE CABOODLE

Serves 2   **Calories** 313   **Simplicity**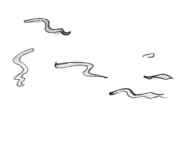

Preparation 15 mins   **Fat** 8g

Cooking 5 mins

1 Prepare the noodles according to the packet instructions, then drain well.

2 Heat the oil in a wok or large, heavy-based frying pan over a high heat. Add the spring onions, garlic, cucumber, corn, tomatoes and ham and stir-fry for 3 minutes or until the vegetables are tender and the tomatoes are beginning to split. Stir in the soy sauce and season.

3 Add the noodles to the vegetable mixture, toss well and stir-fry for 1-2 minutes, until heated through.

125g (4oz) dried egg noodles
2 tsp vegetable oil
2 spring onions, chopped
1 small clove garlic, crushed
75g (3oz) cucumber, cut into thin sticks
2 baby corn, sliced
4 cherry tomatoes
50g (2oz) smoked ham, cut into cubes
1 tbsp light soy sauce
Black pepper

If you're feeling brave, you can add to the fun of this healthy Chinese stir-fry by letting children eat it with chopsticks! But keep the kitchen towels handy!

SCARECROWS

Simplicity

Serves 2

Preparation 20 mins

Cooking 45 mins

Calories 652

Fat 40g

225g (8oz) sweet potatoes, cut into 5mm (¼in) strips

1 tomato, halved

Cooked peas, carrots and courgette for the face (optional)

For the pasties

1 skinless boneless chicken breast, diced

1 tbsp plain flour, seasoned with black pepper

2 tsp vegetable oil, plus extra for deep-frying

1 small leek, finely chopped

1 small clove garlic, crushed

2 button mushrooms, quartered

125ml (4½fl oz) chicken stock

½ tsp dried thyme

100g (3½oz) shortcrust pastry

1 egg, beaten, to glaze

1 To make the pasties, toss the chicken in the flour. Heat the oil in a heavy-based frying pan, add the chicken and cook, stirring, for 5 minutes to brown. Add the leek, garlic and mushrooms and fry for 3 minutes. Add the stock and thyme and simmer, covered, for 20 minutes, until the chicken is cooked.

2 Meanwhile, preheat the oven to 200°C/400°F/ Gas Mark 6. Break off a walnut-sized piece of pastry, roll out to a square on a floured surface, then cut out 2 triangles for the scarecrows' hats. Roll out the remaining pastry to a 25 x 12cm (10 x 5in) rectangle, then cut in half across. Divide the chicken mixture between the halves. Brush the edges with egg, draw up the corners and press to seal. Brush with egg, place on a baking sheet and bake for 20 minutes. Add the hats and cook for a further 10 minutes.

3 Deep-fry the sweet potato for 5-7 minutes, until golden. Drain on kitchen towels. To make each scarecrow, use a pasty for the body, half a tomato for a head and peas, carrot and courgette for the face. Add a hat and use the fries to make hair, arms and a pole.

Children will love these fun chicken pasties. You can use any spare fries to make some flying birds.

SQUIRREL FEASTS

Serves 2

Preparation 25 mins, plus 3 mins standing

Cooking 35 mins

Calories 184

Fat 10g

Simplicity

1 Preheat the oven to 190°C/375°F/Gas Mark 5. Combine the stuffing mix with 1 tablespoon of boiling water, set aside for 3 minutes, then mix in the sausage meat. Open out the chicken thighs and divide the stuffing mixture between them. Roll them up, brush with oil, then secure with cocktail sticks. Sprinkle over the thyme. Place in an ovenproof dish, seam-side down, and roast for 35 minutes or until cooked through and golden.

2 Meanwhile, make the squirrel tails. Cut 2 thin lengthways slices from 1 carrot for the tails. Cut diagonal slits down both sides of each slice, then place in ice-cold water for 15 minutes or until slightly curled. Carve 2 squirrel heads from the remaining carrot. Remove the cocktail sticks from the chicken, place on a plate, lean the carrot tails behind and balance the carrot heads on top. Spoon peas around.

Ingredients
2 tsp parsley and thyme stuffing mix
50g (2oz) pork sausage meat
2 skinless boneless chicken thighs
Olive oil for brushing
¼ tsp dried thyme
2 carrots to garnish
Peas to serve

Make these squirrels as a special treat – they're filled with a delicious herby sausage stuffing. If you're giving them to young children, don't forget to remove the cocktail sticks.

FARM BARN

Simplicity

Serves 4

Preparation 10 mins

Cooking 15 mins

Calories 331

Fat 15g

227g pack fresh breaded chicken goujons

227g pack frozen potato waffles

4 frozen crispy vegetable fingers

4 small tomatoes

Olive oil for roasting

225g (8oz) frozen mixed vegetables

4 tbsp baked beans

1 Preheat the oven to 220°C/425°F/Gas Mark 7. Put the goujons, waffles and vegetable fingers on baking trays and cook for 15 minutes, turning once, until cooked through and golden.

2 Meanwhile, slice the tops off the tomatoes, scoop out the seeds and discard. Sprinkle with oil. Place on a baking tray and cook for 3 minutes or until softened. Cook the vegetables in boiling water for 3-5 minutes, until tender, then drain and keep warm. Heat the beans in a saucepan.

3 Fill the tomatoes with the beans. To assemble the barn, arrange 3 tomatoes on a large plate and stand the waffles upright around them to make 4 walls. Place the vegetable fingers over the waffles for rafters, then arrange the goujons on top to make a roof. Spoon the mixed vegetables around the outside of the 'barn' to hold up the walls and put 1 tomato outside as a plant pot.

Get the children to guess what's inside the barn before they tuck in. You can put mushrooms or anything else you like inside – you don't have to use tomatoes.

ROOKERY COOKERY

Serves 2 **Calories** 369 **Simplicity**

Preparation 20 mins **Fat** 15g

Cooking 20 mins

1 To make the sauce, combine the crème fraîche, mustard and chives, then cover and refrigerate.

2 Preheat the grill to high. Cover the grill pan rack with foil and lightly grease. Mix together the chicken, breadcrumbs, parsley, thyme, brown sauce and half the beaten egg, then season. Shape into 8 'eggs', using your hands. Grill for 5-10 minutes, turning occasionally, until browned.

3 Meanwhile, make the nests. Place the grated potato in a tea towel and squeeze out any excess water. Put into a bowl with the onion, stir in the rest of the beaten egg and season. Divide the mixture in half, shape into rounds and press to flatten slightly. Heat a little oil in a large, heavy-based frying pan. Cook the rounds for 5-6 minutes on each side, until golden.

4 Make a hollow in the centre of each nest, drain them on kitchen towels, then place on plates. Spoon over the sauce, then top each with 4 'eggs'.

Sunflower oil for greasing and frying

150g (5oz) skinless boneless chicken breast, minced

2 tbsp fresh breadcrumbs

1 tbsp chopped fresh parsley

1 tsp dried thyme

1 tsp brown sauce

2 medium eggs, beaten

Black pepper

225g (8oz) waxy potatoes, such as Maris Piper, peeled and grated

1 small onion, finely chopped

For the sauce

1 tbsp crème fraîche

½ tsp mild mustard

2 tsp snipped fresh chives

Hatch a tea-time surprise for children with these golden, crunchy potato nests, topped with a creamy sauce and filled with four delicious bird's eggs.

MAGPIE'S NEST

Simplicity

Serves 2

Preparation 15 mins

Cooking 10 mins

Calories 564

Fat 20g

150g (5oz) dried short-cut macaroni

4 tbsp crème fraîche

1 tsp soft light brown sugar

1 tsp lemon juice

1 tsp light soy sauce

1 tbsp chopped fresh parsley, plus extra leaves to garnish

Black pepper

2 tsp vegetable oil

1 skinless boneless turkey breast steak, cut into thin strips

1 tsp mild mustard

1 small carrot, cut into matchsticks

1 small courgette, cut into matchsticks

1 Cook the macaroni according to the packet instructions, until just firm to the bite. Drain well.

2 Meanwhile, mix together the crème fraîche, sugar, lemon juice, soy sauce and parsley. Season, cover and refrigerate. Heat the oil in a large, heavy-based frying pan or wok, add the turkey strips and mustard and cook for 5 minutes, turning often, until the turkey is cooked through and lightly browned.

3 Add the carrot and courgette to the turkey and stir-fry for 4 minutes or until tender but still crisp. Stir in the macaroni and heat through, then stir in the crème fraîche mixture and heat for 1 minute. Garnish with parsley to serve.

Magpies are always stealing brightly coloured bits and pieces to feather their raggedy nests, and children will love this tasty hoard of turkey strips and crisp vegetables.

PANSIES

Serves 2

Preparation 15 mins

Cooking 30 mins

Calories 157

Fat 3g

Simplicity ♟♟

1 Cook the sweet potato in boiling water for 10 minutes or until tender. Drain well, then mash. Heat the oil in a frying pan, add the spring onions and fry for 3 minutes or until softened.

2 Preheat the grill to medium. Place the sweet potato, spring onions, tuna, sweetcorn, red pepper, Worcestershire sauce and flour in a bowl and mix in the milk. Season, then shape into 4 round cakes with your hands. Brush the tops with oil and grill for 5 minutes. Turn over, brush with oil again and grill for a further 5 minutes or until golden. Drain on kitchen towels and keep warm.

3 Meanwhile, heat 2.5cm (1in) of oil in a large saucepan. Fry the beetroot or carrot slices for 3-5 minutes, until crisp. Drain on kitchen towels. To serve, place 2 fish cakes on each plate and top each cake with 4-5 beetroot or carrot slices to make the pansy petals.

50g (2oz) sweet potato, diced

1 tsp sunflower oil, plus extra for brushing and deep-frying

2 spring onions, finely chopped

100g can tuna in spring water, drained

1 tbsp sweetcorn, drained

½ small red pepper, finely chopped

Dash of Worcestershire sauce

1 tbsp plain flour

1 tbsp full-fat milk

Black pepper

1 small raw beetroot or 1 large carrot, thinly sliced

Brightly coloured beetroot or carrot 'pansies' make a delicious topping for these tasty tuna fish cakes. Serve them with some baby carrots and courgettes.

LITTLE FISHES

Simplicity

Serves 2

Preparation 10 mins

Cooking 50 mins

Calories 592

Fat 24g

100g (3½oz) long-grain rice
1 medium egg
200g (7oz) smoked haddock
200ml (7fl oz) full-fat milk
25g (1oz) cooked peeled prawns, defrosted if frozen
1 tsp lemon juice
Pinch of nutmeg
Pinch of curry powder
1-2 tbsp chopped fresh parsley
3 tbsp single cream
Black pepper
15g (½oz) butter, plus extra for greasing
2 slices of bread
½ lemon, cut into quarters

1 Preheat the oven to 180°C/350°F/Gas Mark 4. Cook the rice according to the packet instructions, then drain. Meanwhile, hard-boil the egg for 10 minutes. Shell under cold water and finely chop. Put the haddock into a saucepan, cover with the milk and poach for 6-8 minutes, until just firm. Drain well, then flake the flesh, removing any bones and skin.

2 Place the egg, fish, rice and prawns in a bowl. Stir in the lemon juice, nutmeg, curry powder, parsley, cream and seasoning. Transfer to a greased ovenproof dish. Dot the butter over the top, cover and cook for 25 minutes.

3 Meanwhile, toast the bread, then cut out fish shapes. Serve the rice dish with lemon wedges and the fish-shaped toasts.

This fishy dishy is made from haddock, prawns and rice. The fish toasts are a great touch and will net you plenty of praise. They're easy to do with a small sharp knife.

STARFISH AND SEA CHEST

Serves 2

Preparation 20 mins

Cooking 35 mins

Calories 538

Fat 29g

Simplicity ♟♟

1 Boil the potato for 10 minutes or until tender, then drain and mash. Place the cod in a saucepan and cover with the milk. Poach for 5 minutes or until firm, then drain and flake, removing any bones.

2 Mix together the mash, cod and parsley and season. Divide the mixture into 2 and mould each half into a star shape, using your hands or a 7.5cm (3in) star-shaped cutter. Dip the starfish into the egg, then the breadcrumbs. Heat 1 tablespoon of the oil in a large, non-stick frying pan and cook the starfish for 5-7 minutes, turning once, until cooked and golden. Drain on kitchen towels and keep warm.

3 Heat the remaining oil in the frying pan, until hot but not smoking. Drain, then dry the chips in a clean tea towel. Fry for 7-10 minutes, until cooked and golden, then drain on kitchen towels.

4 Meanwhile, steam the cabbage for 4-5 minutes until tender. To serve, build a square of chips to make a sea chest, then arrange the 'seaweed' cabbage around the starfish.

100g (3½oz) potato, diced
100g (3½oz) skinless cod fillets
150ml (¼ pint) full-fat milk
1 tbsp finely chopped parsley
Black pepper
1 small egg, beaten
2 tbsp fresh breadcrumbs
3 tbsp sunflower oil
2 medium waxy potatoes, such as Maris Piper, cut into 1cm (½in) thick chips
125g (4oz) green cabbage, finely shredded

Discover the hidden treasures of the ocean: crispy starfish, a sea chest of golden fries and cabbage 'seaweed'.

GREEN AS GRASS

Simplicity

Serves 2

Preparation 15 mins

Cooking 10 mins

Calories 461

Fat 21g

75g (3oz) fine green beans, halved widthways

75g (3oz) frozen chopped spinach, defrosted

150g (5oz) dried tagliatelle verde

2 tsp olive oil

Knob of butter

1 clove garlic, crushed

3 tbsp crème fraîche

½ tsp pesto

2 tbsp freshly grated Parmesan, plus extra to sprinkle

Black pepper

2 tsp full-fat milk

1 tbsp chopped fresh parsley

1 Boil the green beans in a little water for 5-6 minutes, until cooked but still crunchy. Drain. Squeeze out any excess water from the spinach. Cook the tagliatelle according to the packet instructions, until just firm to the bite, then drain.

2 Meanwhile, heat the oil and butter in a saucepan, add the garlic and cook for 1 minute to soften. Stir in the crème fraîche, pesto, spinach and Parmesan and heat through for 1 minute. Add the beans and heat for a further 1 minute, then season.

3 Add the pasta to the pan, then stir in the milk and most of the parsley. Toss well and heat through. Pile into bowls, sprinkle with Parmesan and garnish with the remaining parsley.

Most children love pasta and this dish is a great way to get them to eat their 'greens'. If they refuse to eat spinach, try replacing it with some broccoli florets.

AUTUMN TWIGS AND LEAVES

Serves 2

Preparation 20 mins

Cooking 25 mins

Calories 455

Fat 34g

Simplicity

1 Preheat the oven to 190°C/375°F/Gas Mark 5. Put the pumpkin, pepper, onion and tomatoes into a roasting tin. Sprinkle with the oil and balsamic vinegar and roast in the centre of the oven for 25 minutes or until soft and slightly browned, turning once.

2 Meanwhile, make the twigs. Lay the puff pastry on a floured surface and cut into 1cm (½in) strips. Place on a greased baking sheet and sprinkle with the cheese. Bake at the top of the oven for 10 minutes or until crisp and golden.

3 To make the dressing, mix together the mayonnaise, mustard, garlic and seasoning. To serve, arrange the salad leaves and roasted vegetables on small plates. Serve with spoonfuls of the dressing and the cheesy twigs.

For the 'leaves'

125g (4oz) pumpkin, peeled and cut into chunks

1 small yellow pepper, deseeded and cut into chunks

1 small red onion, quartered

4 cherry tomatoes

2 tsp olive oil, plus extra for greasing

1 tsp balsamic vinegar

50g (2oz) mixed salad leaves

For the 'twigs'

100g (3½oz) ready-rolled puff pastry

25g (1oz) Cheddar, finely grated

For the dressing

2 tbsp mayonnaise

½ tsp wholegrain mustard

1 small clove garlic, crushed

Black pepper

This salad of warm roasted vegetables is a real favourite when it's served with cheese sticks and a tangy dressing.

OLD BANGER

Simplicity

Serves 2

Preparation 20 mins

Cooking 1 hr 15 mins

Calories 394

Fat 18g

1 large potato, cut into 1cm (½in) slices

1 tbsp vegetable oil

½ onion, chopped

4 vegetarian sausages, halved widthways

1 small parsnip, sliced

1 eating apple, peeled, cored and sliced

1 small carrot, sliced

1 small courgette, sliced

1 tbsp tomato purée

200ml (7fl oz) vegetable stock

100ml (4fl oz) apple juice

Black pepper

1 tbsp full-fat milk

1 Preheat the oven to 190°C/375°F/Gas Mark 5. Boil the potato slices for 10-15 minutes, until just tender, then drain. Meanwhile, heat the oil in a heavy-based frying pan. Add the onion and sausages and fry for 5 minutes or until the onion has softened and the sausages have browned.

2 Add the parsnip, apple, carrot, courgette, tomato purée, vegetable stock and apple juice, then stir well. Season, then transfer to an ovenproof dish. Arrange the potato slices over the top and brush with milk. Cook, covered, for 40 minutes. Raise the heat to 220°C/425°F/Gas Mark 7, then uncover and cook for another 20 minutes to brown the potato.

Most children love sausages of any description, and both meat and vegetarian ones go really well with this fruity vegetable hotpot and its lid of crispy potatoes.

CHEESY FEET PIE

Serves 4

Preparation 20 mins

Cooking 1 hr

Calories 257

Fat 11g

Simplicity

1 Heat the butter in a frying pan, then add the onion and cook for 5 minutes or until softened. Add the garlic, parsnip and carrot and cook for a further 5 minutes until softened slightly. Add the lentils, tomatoes, herbs, vegetable stock and pepper to the pan and cook gently for 25 minutes, stirring occasionally, until the vegetables are tender. Preheat the oven to 200°C/400°F/Gas Mark 6.

2 Meanwhile, make the 'cheesy feet' scones. Sift the flour and mustard into a bowl. Rub the butter into the flour mixture with your fingertips until it resembles fine breadcrumbs. Add the Cheddar and soured cream, then mix with a fork to form a dough. Knead on a floured surface until pliable. Press or roll out to a thickness of 1cm (½in), then shape into feet.

3 Spoon the vegetable mixture into an ovenproof dish. Place the scone feet on top, then brush with beaten egg. Bake for 25 minutes or until the feet are well risen.

15g (½oz) butter

1 small onion, finely chopped

1 small clove garlic, crushed

1 small parsnip, finely chopped

1 small carrot, finely chopped

100g (3½oz) canned green lentils, drained and rinsed

227g can chopped tomatoes

1 tsp dried mixed herbs

4 tbsp vegetable stock

Black pepper

For the 'cheesy feet'

100g (3½oz) self-raising flour

Pinch of dry mustard

15g (½oz) chilled butter, cubed

25g (1oz) Cheddar, grated

4 tbsp soured cream

1 small egg, beaten, to glaze

Who's been walking in my pie? Children will adore this winter-warming vegetable and lentil pie, topped with its ingeniously shaped cheesy footprints.

HOP SCOTCH

Simplicity

Serves 4

Preparation 10 mins
plus 2 hrs freezing and
20 mins cooling

Calories 533

Fat 27g

100g (3½oz) butterscotch sweets

500g tub vanilla ice cream

312g can mandarins, drained

3 chocolate flakes

1 Put the butterscotch sweets into a strong plastic bag. Roughly crush with a rolling pin.

2 Place the ice cream in a large bowl and mash with a fork. Mix in the crushed butterscotch. Return to the container and freeze for 1-2 hours.

3 Transfer the ice cream to the fridge for 20 minutes before serving to soften slightly. Place the mandarins in sundae glasses, together with 2 scoops of ice cream. Crush one of the chocolate flakes and sprinkle over the top of the ice cream. Cut the remaining flakes in half and push 1 into each serving.

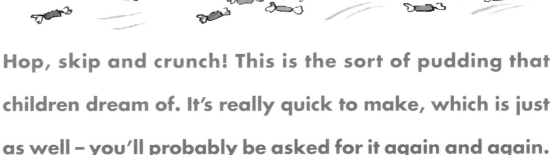

Hop, skip and crunch! This is the sort of pudding that children dream of. It's really quick to make, which is just as well – you'll probably be asked for it again and again.

APPLE ROLL-UPS

Serves 2

Preparation 15 mins

plus 20 mins resting

Cooking 25 mins

Calories 348

Fat 18g

Simplicity

1 To make the batter, blend the flour, milk, egg, orange rind and melted butter until smooth in a food processor or using a hand blender. Leave it to rest for 20 minutes.

2 Meanwhile, make the filling. Put the apples, cinnamon and 1 tablespoon of water into a small saucepan, cover, and cook gently for 5-7 minutes, stirring occasionally, until the apples have softened.

3 Melt just enough butter to cover the base of a 18cm (7in) non-stick frying pan. Pour in a quarter of the batter and tilt the pan so that it covers the base. Cook for 1-2 minutes on each side, until golden. Keep warm and repeat to make 3 more pancakes, greasing the pan when necessary.

4 Place 2 pancakes on each plate. Fill with the apple mixture and carefully roll up. Serve with maple syrup.

50g (2oz) plain flour

150ml (¼ pint) full-fat milk

1 medium egg

Finely grated rind of ½ small orange

25g (1oz) butter, melted, plus extra for frying

Maple syrup to serve

For the filling

2 eating apples, peeled, cored and chopped

½ tsp ground cinnamon

Roll up, roll up... for these hot apple-filled pancakes, served with maple syrup. Try them with a generous dollop of creamy yogurt or a scoop of vanilla ice cream.

SHRUBBERY

Simplicity

Serves 4

Preparation 10 mins
plus 2 hrs cooling
and 10 hrs chilling

Calories 90

Fat trace

135g pack green jelly
1 tbsp lemon yogurt
200g (7oz) soft fruit such as raspberries, blackberries and strawberries

1 Make the jelly as directed on the packet, but with 500ml (18fl oz) water. Cool for 2 hours, then refrigerate for 1-2 hours, until almost set. Whisk in the yogurt, then place in the fridge for 8 hours or until set.

2 Cut the jelly into cubes, dipping the knife into water to stop the jelly sticking. Pile the cubes into bowls, then scatter the fruit over the top.

On sunny summer days, this fruity pudding makes a healthy and refreshing treat. Children love the colourful mixture of berries and citrus-flavoured jelly chunks.

HEDGEROW PIE

Serves 2

Preparation 25 mins

plus 5 mins cooling

Cooking 30 mins

Calories 437

Fat 26g

Simplicity

1 Preheat the oven to 200°C/400°F/Gas Mark 6. Put the fruit and sugar into a saucepan. Simmer, covered, for 1-2 minutes, until the fruit begins to soften, then leave for 5 minutes to cool. Strain the fruit, reserving the juice.

2 Set aside a small piece of pastry to make the decorations. Roll out the remaining pastry on a floured surface into a rough circle, about 18cm (7in) across. Place on a non-stick baking sheet. Put the fruit in the centre of the pastry and gather up the edges, leaving the top slightly open. Brush the top of the pastry with a little of the egg.

3 Roll out the reserved pastry and cut out acorn, leaf and blackberry shapes. Brush the shapes with egg and stick them onto the sides of the pie. Bake for 25 minutes or until the pastry is golden. Remove from the oven. Lightly dust with caster sugar. Serve with the reserved fruit juice, if liked.

250g (9oz) fresh or frozen mixed fruits, such as blackberries, raspberries, blueberries and strawberries

25g (1oz) caster sugar, plus extra for dusting

150g (5oz) shortcrust pastry

1 egg, beaten, for glazing

This fruit pie is delicious and great fun to make. Children will love it even more if you let them go berry picking and help you make the pastry decorations.

BANANA DRAMA

Simplicity

Serves 2

Preparation 5 mins

Cooking 8 mins

Calories 244

Fat 10g

25g (1oz) butter

1 eating apple, peeled, cored and sliced

2 bananas, thickly sliced

Finely grated rind of ¼ lemon and ½ tsp lemon juice

25g (1oz) soft light brown sugar

¼ tsp ground cinnamon

1 Melt the butter in a medium-sized saucepan. Add the apple and cook over a medium heat for 3 minutes, turning once, until softened. Add the bananas, stir gently, and cook for a further 2 minutes or until golden.

2 Add the lemon rind and juice, sugar and cinnamon to the pan. Cook for 2-3 minutes, stirring gently, until the sauce turns golden and coats the fruit.

Hot, gooey caramel sauce poured over chunks of banana and slices of sticky apple – it's guaranteed to get children eating fruit. Serve it with some vanilla ice cream.

STICKY RICE SANDCASTLES

Serves 2

Preparation 5 mins
plus 10 mins cooling and
1 hr chilling

Cooking 50 mins

Calories 477

Fat 16g

Simplicity ♟♟

1 Lightly grease 2 x 150ml (¼ pint) moulds or ramekins. Put the rice in a saucepan and cover with 150ml (¼ pint) of water. Bring to the boil, then reduce the heat and simmer, covered, for 4-5 minutes, until the water is absorbed.

2 Heat the milk in a saucepan. Add the milk to the rice with the butter, lemon rind, sugar and cinnamon. Simmer, uncovered, over a low heat, stirring occasionally, for 40 minutes or until the mixture is thick and creamy.

3 Spoon the rice into the moulds or ramekins. Cool for 10 minutes, then refrigerate for 1 hour or until set. Preheat the grill to medium. Run a knife around the edge of each pudding and turn out onto a baking sheet. Sprinkle the tops with a layer of brown sugar and grill for 1 minute or until the sugar caramelises. Serve on individual plates, with a sprinkling of brown sugar for the sand.

25g (1oz) butter, plus extra for greasing

75g (3oz) short-grain or pudding rice

300ml (½ pint) full-fat milk

Grated rind of ½ lemon

75g (3oz) caster sugar

Pinch of cinnamon

Soft light brown sugar to decorate

Decorate these sticky 'sandcastles' with colourful flags by gluing triangles of tissue paper to cocktail sticks. Don't leave the sticks for small children to play with though.

SWEET LITTLE BONFIRES

Simplicity

Makes 36

Preparation 15 mins
plus 4 mins cooling

Cooking 15 mins

Calories 93

Fat 4g

125g (4oz) dried mixed fruit

60g (2¼oz) corn flakes

100g (3½oz) Shredded Wheat, crushed (about 4 biscuits)

100g (3½oz) glacé cherries, chopped

175ml (6fl oz) condensed milk

150g (5oz) desiccated coconut

150g (5oz) milk chocolate

1 Preheat the oven to 160°C/325°F/Gas Mark 3. Line 3 baking sheets with baking or rice paper. Combine the dried mixed fruit, corn flakes, Shredded Wheat, cherries, condensed milk and coconut in a large bowl. Press the mixture into little mounds and place on the baking sheets, spacing them evenly. Bake for 15 minutes or until golden and crisp.

2 Meanwhile, melt the chocolate in a bowl placed over a saucepan of simmering water. Remove the 'bonfires' from the oven and leave for 2 minutes to cool slightly. Drizzle over the melted chocolate and cool for a further 1-2 minutes before serving.

These are great to hand around on Bonfire Night, and can be made by children without too much supervision. But be warned, they'll disappear faster than a rocket!

MUDDY PUDDLES

Makes 4

Preparation 20 mins
plus 20 mins chilling
and 15 mins cooling

Cooking 25 mins

Calories 397

Fat 28g

Simplicity

1 Put the biscuits into a plastic bag, seal, then crush with a rolling pin. Melt 25g (1oz) of the butter in a saucepan. Remove from the heat and mix in the biscuits. Line a muffin tin with 4 paper muffin cases. Divide the biscuit mixture between them, pressing over the base and sides of each case with the back of a teaspoon. Refrigerate for 20 minutes or until firm.

2 Preheat the oven to 180°C /350°F/Gas Mark 4. Meanwhile, put the remaining butter, plain chocolate and syrup into a bowl set over a saucepan of simmering water. Heat gently, stirring, until melted. Remove from the heat and cool for 5 minutes. Whisk in the egg and vanilla essence.

3 Spoon the chocolate mixture over the biscuit bases and bake for 20 minutes or until just firm. Leave to cool for 10 minutes. Meanwhile, melt the white chocolate in a bowl set over a pan of simmering water, then drizzle over the puddles.

Ingredients
75g (3oz) chocolate digestive biscuits
75g (3oz) butter
75g (3oz) plain chocolate
2 tbsp golden syrup
1 medium egg, beaten
Few drops of vanilla essence
15g (½oz) white chocolate

Chocoholic children (or adults) will adore these pools of chocolate. They've got a chocolate biscuit base, a creamy chocolate filling and even more drizzled on top. Heaven!

LIQUID LIME

Simplicity

Serves 4

Preparation 20 mins

Cooking 45 mins

Calories 234

Fat 10g

25g (1oz) butter, plus extra for greasing
100g (3½oz) caster sugar
Finely grated rind and juice of 2 limes
150ml (¼ pint) full-fat milk
2 medium eggs, separated
25g (1oz) self-raising flour

1 Preheat the oven to 190°C/375°F/ Gas Mark 5. Beat the butter and sugar together. Add the lime rind and juice and beat well. Mix the milk and egg yolks in a separate bowl, then add to the creamed mixture with the flour and beat well.

2 Whisk the egg whites until they form stiff peaks (this is easiest with an electric whisk). Fold a spoonful into the creamed mixture to loosen it, then fold in the rest. Pour into a buttered 1 litre (1¾ pint) soufflé dish.

3 Place the dish on a double layer of newspaper in a deep roasting tin. Pour boiling water into the tin to reach halfway up the sides. Cook for 45 minutes, until well risen and firm.

A light spongy top hides a luscious liquid lime custard underneath. It's wonderful served warm with some cream, but don't hang around if you want to get a look in.

PARSNIP PASSION

Makes 24

Preparation 30 mins
plus 35 mins cooling

Cooking 20 mins

Calories 212 each

Fat 9g each

Simplicity

1 Preheat the oven to 180°C/350°F/Gas Mark 4. Using a wooden spoon, combine the flour, caster and brown sugar, baking powder, bicarbonate of soda, cinnamon and salt. Add the oil and eggs and beat until thoroughly combined. Mix in the parsnips and pineapple and beat well.

2 Spoon the mixture into paper cases in 2 bun trays and bake for 15-20 minutes, until firm and golden. Cool for a few minutes, then remove from the trays and set aside for 30 minutes or until cool. Meanwhile, make the icing. Mix the icing sugar, mascarpone, lemon juice and vanilla essence with a fork until smooth. Spread over the cakes.

3 Cut out mini parsnip shapes from the yellow fondant icing. Pare strips of green fondant with a vegetable peeler, then twist round a clean pencil to curl. Gently slip the curls off the pencil and set aside to dry. Arrange the parsnips on top of the cakes.

225g (8oz) self-raising flour

75g (3oz) caster sugar

75g (3oz) soft light brown sugar

1 tsp baking powder

1 tsp bicarbonate of soda

½ tsp ground cinnamon

½ tsp salt

150ml (¼ pint) sunflower oil

2 medium eggs, beaten

125g (4oz) parsnips, grated

200g (7oz) canned crushed pineapple, drained

For the icing

275g (10oz) icing sugar, sifted

125g (4oz) mascarpone

4 tsp lemon juice

2 drops vanilla essence

1 box coloured fondant icing

This is a variation of the ever-popular carrot cake. Children love the natural sweetness of parsnips and pineapple and they can help make the tiny parsnips that go on top.

INDEX

The Tesco Cookery Series

Fast Family Meals • Great Value Meals • Fast Fresh Food • Fun Food for Children
Pasta • Fish and Shellfish • Mainly Vegetables • Meat and Poultry • Puddings
Best of British • Mediterranean Food • Tastes of the Orient

The Lifestyle Collection

Cooking for Health • Entertaining • The Essential Cookbook • Food for Friends